This Wasn't in the Parenting Books

Real Life Coaching Lessons for Moms Who Are Overwhelmed, Overstimulated, and Over It

Dedication

I would like to dedicate this book, first and foremost, to my life coaches, Stephanie and Lila, for helping me see things differently—and not making me feel insane when I kind of was.

To my husband, Gary: thank you for supporting my decision to work with a coach without question. You never once said it was too much money or asked, "Why even bother?" Even when it looked like nothing was helping, you continued to support me—and still do.

And finally, to my three wild children—Tamir, Aviva, and Amari—who are both the best things ever and also the bringers of chaos into my life (for now). I love you more than words can say—and I've lost my mind more times than I can count because of the thoughts you've stirred in me.

Here's to growing and expanding—as a person, a mother, a wife, and a professional. Thank you all.

Table of Contents

Introduction

Hi. My name is Asya. I'm a mom of three kids. I've never called myself "calm"—certainly not "cool" or "collected." But motherhood took that to a whole new level. It made sure whatever crazy was buried deep inside me came to the surface. Apparently, motherhood decided I had it too easy.

The first year of motherhood? That was a piece of cake. I ate that sh*t up and asked for seconds. I loved it! I was so excited to be a mother, and having a little baby who mostly slept, nursed, and looked adorable didn't feel too hard. I co-slept, which made nights manageable. We used cloth diapers, which were surprisingly easy with breastmilk poop. Honestly, I looked forward to washing them—they came out smelling milky sweet. Yum! I even enjoyed the ritual of folding them. I loved babywearing and taking walks with my baby in the carrier once I got the hang of it. Ahh, it was all good.

I was lucky enough to choose when to return to work—not because I had paid maternity leave, but because my husband was supportive and didn't mind me staying home. He also had almost two months off work, which was amazing. I spent my days with a sweet-smelling baby tied to me in a wrap, and it was all so new, so fresh, so exciting.

When he got a little older, things got harder. The walks I had cherished became challenging. He wouldn't sit still in the stroller or the wrap. I could no longer relax and watch a show while breastfeeding. He began to have opinions—and tantrums. Oh my God, the tantrums! I had no idea how to handle them.

But I had already planned to have three kids, spaced two years apart. So by the time the chaos started, I was already pregnant with the second. And yes, there were moments when I wondered, *Why am I doing this again—with this little monster running around?* But that was the plan. And now that they're 3.5, 6, and 8 (at the time I'm writing this), I'm so happy they have each other—and that I have all three. It's not that I regret anything, but I do wish I had more tools from the start. More support. I still wish for that.

"Hard" doesn't even begin to describe how things got once my sweet baby became a toddler. And then, adding a newborn to the mix? Oh no. No, no, no, no—I was not okay. All of this to say, I wasn't prepared. Nothing could have really prepared me, I don't think. I read the books, I learned so much about parenting, but what I did not learn is how to manage my mind about this all. My mind was, and in many ways, still is, a wild monkey swinging from tree to tree completely untamed.

None of the books I had read were focused on the mother, and I probably didn't even think of investigating something like that at the time, but I was already pretty into self-development and self-help books. So, it's not like I was completely unfamiliar. I was probably at least as, if not more, familiar with self-help concepts than most. But none of it was helpful. Not at that time when my life had completely been torn apart by little people in ways I could never have expected.

At this time, I was getting most of my daily dopamine from buying, selling, and trading baby wraps. It was an enjoyable hobby of mine and wraps were something I used daily, multiple times a day, they were very useful. Often, I would talk to the moms I was buying, selling, or trading with (BST, as it's called) and made one of my best friends (hi, Anna!) this way.

One day, I was talking to a mom who mentioned she had five kids. Five. Five children! Wow! Her youngest was about 6 months older than my oldest. As I often did, I saw an opportunity and I took it. I asked her how she handles five kids and what is her advice to stay sane because I was drowning with my two. She told me a few things and then said that she is a life coach. I found the name kind of funny. Like…you teach people how to do "life"? What does that even mean? Like how to use a planner and cook eggs? I had no idea.

I asked more questions to try and understand, and she explained a little more and told me she could offer me a free session to see what it's all about. I gladly took it. I found this session to be very interesting and helpful. She offered me one more. I was planning on just taking the free sessions and calling it a day. But it was really interesting stuff. And really unlike anything I've heard or read before. After that, she offered me a 6-session package for $600 (her prices have increased since then). I had a really hard time with the price and couldn't decide. She said it's because I don't trust myself enough and I have a scarcity mindset. Both things were true. It just seemed like a huge investment, and I wasn't sure it was worth it. But something in me pushed me to say, "Yes" and I did. I swore to myself it would just be the 6 sessions and I'd be done. But like any true drug addict, that is not what happened.

I bought more and more sessions. When she drastically raised her prices, I looked for a new life coach. I quickly learned that not all life coaches were created equally. Some are about as good as the advice you'd get from a Facebook group. I realized that what made my original coach so good was the particular training program she went through called "The Life Coach School." I did find another life coach who also trained there and was equally impressed. I concluded that this is *the* school that teaches in a way that is just, honestly, mind-blowing. I ended up coming back to the original life coach, but after years of coaching, I know these lessons inside out. I just need reminders and to talk through certain situations.

Here are the things I learned that I have never been taught anywhere else.

I have tried to divide each concept up into a chapter for organization purposes, however, all the ideas intertwine and overlap and most of them bear repeating.

Note: I am not a life coach or an expert. I have not mastered everything here; I am not a blissed-out mom who never has a problem. I am, however, someone who has learned a lot and wants to share some really practical lessons that go far beyond anything else I found. I have looked elsewhere and found nothing close to what my life coach offered. I was searching for something that isn't a band-aid but addressed a lot of the real struggles in parenthood that most people don't talk about. I am not afraid to admit how difficult it is and not sugar coat it, but I am also unwilling to settle for "it is what it is" and be miserable. I hope you find these just as valuable as I did and above all else, I hope you enjoy them!

As a side note, I wrote this book fairly quickly, but then I took a long time to release it. I finally decided I'm doing it and decided to edit it closer to the publishing date, so a few details have since changed. You'll particularly notice this in my kids' ages if you know me personally. I was going to fix this detail, but it doesn't really change the content of this book, now does it?

Our Thoughts Create Our Results

This statement hit me like a ton of bricks. This was our first lesson and the premise behind all of our coaching. What the hell is that supposed to mean? I was a brand-new mom, with a toddler and a newborn. And let me tell you, that combo is not for the faint of heart. My goal was always to have three kids, spaced two years apart. I had no clue what that actually entailed, or how hard it would be, it was just this "dream" based on what I saw in other families. Two years apart seemed like a perfect choice because they'd be close in age, best friends, and frolicking into the sunset together or whatever. I didn't really think through the logistics. My toddler was 23 months old when I had my second baby. 23 months apart. Did I truly understand what a 23-month-old was and how far from independent they would be? No. And on top of that, I was adding the responsibility of a newborn. Did I think about how I'd manage both? Nope. I was too focused on the "closeness" and the "friendship."

To be fair, now that they're 8 and 6 (with a 3.5-year-old in the mix), it's true. This age gap is great from their perspective. The 8-year-old teaches the 6-year-old a lot, but they still play together. It's sweet, and I'm so happy things worked out this way. But— BUT—I would never recommend having kids this close together. It was a nightmare. So. Hard. I was overwhelmed. So, when I learned that my thoughts, not my circumstances, were creating my results, I almost fainted. I was stunned by how absurd that sounded. Yet, at the same time, it gave me a weird sense of permission to complain. I felt so guilty about how hard things were because it "should've" been such a wonderful time in my life. Why wasn't I appreciating it all? But it wasn't the circumstances, it was my thoughts.

It's not the kids. It's not the husband. It's not the to-do list or the pile of laundry or the job or the mother-in-law.
It's not the house. It's not your clutter. It's not your baby who is not sleeping.
It's your thoughts about all of it.

This is good news. Because we can't control our circumstances all the time. We can't control the kids, the house, the finances, the people around us, the comments, the interruptions. But we can control our thoughts. That's where our power lies.

The concept was explained to me using *The Model*. It looks like this:

Circumstances (This is always an objective fact, like "the baby is crying")

Thought (This is the thought about it, like "I can't stand this noise!")

Feeling (This is the feeling that comes up in your body, like dread)

Action (This is what you do as a result of the thought, like covering your ears and crying)

Result (This is what happens because of your actions, like ignoring the baby and the crying getting worse)

We filled in example after example. Here's one:

Circumstance: You only got 4 hours of sleep last night.

Thought: "I am so tired!"

Feeling: Resentment at your life.

Action: You complain, drink coffee (which makes you jittery), and cry.

Result: You're even more tired because you spent all that mental energy complaining.

"Absolutely not. I completely disagree. This is beyond stupid," I thought. And yet, it's true. Trust me when I say, I thought about this *over and over*. I found all kinds of examples where circumstances *did* matter. Of course, some situations are better than others. I still feel that way, but I also realize that circumstances aren't objective truths. They're neutral, and we give them meaning. Now, if that doesn't sound like a load of crap, I don't know what does. And yet, I believe it. My brain still argues with me, but I know it's true. It's not about your location or what's happening to you. It's about how you think about it and interpret it. It's like being pregnant—one person sees it as the greatest joy; another might feel doom and dread. Same circumstance: you're pregnant. The meaning we attach is what makes the difference.

A person could seem to have it all—riches, fame, fortune—and still feel deeply unsatisfied. Meanwhile, someone in far worse circumstances could be genuinely grateful just to be alive.

We all have different feelings, filters, and interpretations of everything, and they come from so many places. The way we were raised plays a role. How our parents reacted to things. Past experiences—like surviving a car accident or having a health scare that turned out to be fine—can shift your perspective. This isn't just "perspective" though. Telling someone they need a "perspective shift" doesn't tell them what to do in the moment. But explaining that it's our thoughts creating our feelings and results? Now *that* gives us something concrete we can change.

Triggers are a perfect example. "Triggered" is a buzzword these days, but it's useful. What might be completely neutral to one person can send another into a downward spiral. The difference isn't in the circumstance—it's in the thoughts each person has.

Another example: the mood difference. When you're in a good mood, food tastes better, you assume the best of what people say, and your kids' whining doesn't bother you as much. When you're in a bad mood, the exact same circumstances—whining kids, someone's bad day—feel completely different. Why? Your thoughts!

So, why does this matter? Why is this worth mentioning?

I believe this concept is the foundation for any change you want to make in your life. If you don't like how you're feeling, or if you don't like certain things in your life (and I'd bet that's 99.9999% of people), then understanding *how* to change it is crucial. Thought work, as it's called, gives us access to the very thing that dictates our feelings. No, it's not always easy to spot what thoughts are creating distress but knowing you have more power than you thought is huge.

One big argument I had against this was: If it's all about thoughts, why bother changing your circumstances at all? The answer: because you want to. Think about that for a minute. You change things because you want to, not because you have to, need to, or should. You do it because *you want to*.

I'm not claiming to have this all figured out. I'm not blissfully happy 24/7. I still want different circumstances sometimes. But I strive for this: I strive to care about my circumstances a lot less. I want to be able to tell my circumstances to "go to hell" and not think twice about them. To me, that's true power.

This idea is also echoed in the world of manifestation. One manifestation YouTuber I follow, Free Tea, said, "Don't let the 3D bully you," the 3D being your circumstances. Your mind is where you really live, and your circumstances are just hanging out there. It's not the scope of this book, but I want to emphasize that this isn't a novel idea. It's the foundation of cognitive behavioral therapy too. You can change your thoughts to change your life.

Sometimes, the thought you need to change is buried so deep, it's hard to find. That's where a brain dump can help. I used to start my coaching sessions by pouring out all my feelings, no matter how jumbled they seemed. My coach would write it all down and then pinpoint the core thought holding everything together, often something like "I'm not worthy." Once you spot the thought, it's much easier to examine it and see what needs to change. Our brains often default to the same familiar thoughts, which have been etched in over time. So, in vulnerable moments, your brain will go straight back to those old paths. For me, it's often the thought, "I'm not good enough."

Once you identify that thought, the goal is to change it. Replace it with a new one that turns things around—or at least makes a small shift. It might be hard to jump from "I'm not worthy" to "I'm amazing!" but you can start smaller: "I am worthy." This is the basis of affirmations. You don't have to go from feeling awful to feeling amazing right away, but neutral is a great start.

You can use a "bridge thought" that's not your ultimate belief, but something you can believe now. For example, if you think, "I hate my body," you might start with, "I have a body." That's neutral. Eventually, you might move to, "My body is amazing," but that might feel like too much right now.

Neutrality is easier to reach than joy when you're coming from a place of sadness. Even a slight shift in your thoughts can make a world of difference.

My coach used to say, "Nothing has gone wrong here." I'd roll my eyes. But now I get it. It's not earth-shattering, but it helps settle things and puts your mind in a more neutral state—if you let it.

As the great poet Taylor Swift once said, "Karma is a relaxing thought." Thoughts have that power.

I love affirmations because they let you choose new beliefs. By changing your thoughts, you change your beliefs—and that's powerful stuff! If you constantly think, "Money is hard to come by," guess what? It will be. But when you start believing something else, things will shift. You'll approach money, work, and business in new ways.

There's so much more to say about this, but if you're interested, check out some manifestation content on YouTube.

Same goes for your body. If you believe you're hot stuff, you'll carry yourself that way—and that will confirm your belief.

Your thoughts create your beliefs—and you get to change them.

You are not gaslighting yourself by shifting your thoughts. You are giving yourself relief. You are stepping into power. You're not saying, "This is fine." You're saying, "I get to decide how I experience this."

And that is where change begins.

This brings me to my next point...

You Choose Your Own Thoughts

This bears repeating, over and over again: Your thoughts are not the ultimate truth. They are not predictions, and they do not tell you exactly what will or won't happen. They are simply the result of habits, your subconscious, and ultimately, your beliefs.

Anytime I'm not feeling great, or I'm just a little tired, it's really easy for me to get triggered. And my go-to thoughts when I get triggered? They're all about my worthiness. "I'm not worthy. Someone else is better. I'm not doing enough," etc. Does that make it true? No, not at all. And I *know* that. But it sure feels true. My brain is so good at latching on and taking me along for the ride. I basically have a midlife crisis anytime I'm triggered—and it sucks!

What's your go-to horrible thought pattern? Where does your mind go when things don't go according to plan? A common one people struggle with is related to their body image. I've definitely been there myself.

I've started to notice similar thought patterns in my kids, even at their young age. Our minds love repetition and the comfort of well-worn paths. For example, my 8-year-old might default to thinking, "She always takes my things without asking!" about his sister—even when that's totally untrue. But that doesn't matter to him.

Here's the thing, though: these thoughts are optional. Yes, you can choose to opt in or out of them. Of course, that doesn't mean it's easy. But it is that simple.

I love comparing this to learning a foreign language. I use this analogy a lot because it's such a great way to explain the process.

Currently, I'm learning Polish (I have since switched languages, but again, unimportant details!), which is a difficult language because of its grammar and pronunciation. I have an advantage since I speak Russian, but even then, the pronunciation is tough. I've been using an app called Pimsleur, which I love, though sadly it has very limited Polish lessons. It repeats the same phrases often, which is helpful for learning. What amazes me is that in the beginning, everything sounds awkward. It feels like the human mouth isn't meant to make those sounds. But after hearing the same phrase 50 times, it starts to sound pretty freaking natural! Suddenly, what seemed crazy now makes perfect sense.

That's exactly what a new belief or thought is like. Of course, it doesn't feel natural to say, "I'm amazing, I'm so rich, I'm so successful, parenting is so easy, my kids always listen," because you're not used to it. And you may argue, "But that's objectively not true!" But is it really? Do we ever question our usual thoughts? No, we don't. But we absolutely should.

When your brain offers up a thought like, "This is so hard," we rarely question it. We just accept it as fact. We think, "But it *is* hard!" Is it really? Would everyone in the world agree that it's 100% objectively hard? Would no one disagree? Let's imagine, for the sake of argument, that there's a mother who wanted children more than anything and struggled to conceive for years. When she finally has kids, she's grateful for every moment—even those that others might label "hard." So, there's at least one person who doesn't view it as hard.

I'm not saying you should gaslight yourself into believing your feelings aren't valid. *They are valid*. Yes, it feels hard right now. But what I want to point out is that this is not an objective truth, and it can and should be questioned, just like we question everything else.

As we discussed earlier, we can — and should — implant the thoughts we want. Think of it like in the movie *Inception*, where you deliberately plant an idea in someone's mind. It's an idea that serves you, and it becomes a new belief. If you're not quite ready to do that, at the very least, I want you to know that you don't have to believe every thought that crosses your mind. You don't have to latch on to it and go spiraling down with it. You get to observe the thought and let it go like a balloon you never want to see again.

These recurring thoughts also offer us valuable insight into what's lurking in the shadows of our minds. They show us what we need to release and change. For example, if your thought pattern always defaults to being afraid to put yourself out there, you now know what to work on. But just remember, it's not an ultimate truth.

Life Is 50/50

One day, I was complaining to my coach about where I live, feeling uninspired by it all. Both my husband and I grew up in the Chicago suburbs. I studied abroad in France, lived in Shanghai for two years, traveled extensively, and loved it all! Compared to those awe-inspiring places, the Chicago suburbs felt… blah. I always found it incredibly boring and hated the weather and the flatness that stretched as far as I could see. But despite all my travels, my family was always here. And now they've moved away, but his family is still around. Plus, moving to a new country involves a ton of logistics. I started to feel like we were stuck here forever — trapped.

As I discussed this with my coach, she said, "Life is 50/50. If it weren't this, you'd find something else to complain about." And I remember feeling a weight lift off my shoulders. I get how that might not be what everyone wants to hear, but for me, it was incredibly liberating.

It made me realize the truth in her words. Let's say I lived in my dream location, which has always been somewhere in Europe— maybe in a picturesque village, with everything within walking distance, the Mediterranean Sea close by, mild weather year-round, and a beautiful, romantic language spoken around me. Doesn't that sound amazing? I would still find something to complain about. It's true. How many times have we blamed one thing as the root of our problems, only to find that when that issue is resolved, we don't automatically become blissfully happy? Maybe for a little while, but that happiness doesn't last. Why? Because life is 50/50. And that's okay.

I love this concept because it frees me from expectations. But I need constant reminders of it because it's not ingrained in me yet. We're never really taught this: life doesn't have to be perfect all the time. There's real freedom in that. It doesn't mean life can't be perfect—it can be exactly what you make of it. But our problem lies in the expectation of more. More from our careers, more from parenting, more from our "youth," or more from our marriages. I'm all for having high expectations, but I'm often disappointed when things don't live up to them. This doesn't mean you shouldn't have standards or want better things in life. It just means letting go of the overwhelming pressure to make every moment feel super meaningful or to make every part of your life exceptional.

It also means freedom from the attitude of "life is just terrible and it is what it is." I can't stand that phrase because it carries no weight and is used way too often without meaning anything.

Here's another thing: all the people I envy—yes, I have a serious envy problem—are also living the same 50/50 rule. There are joyous moments and not-so-joyous ones. And that's just life. We all experience it.

Doesn't that level the playing field? Doesn't it feel good knowing that everyone has their own 50/50 struggles? It's normal. It's not just you. Sure, some people face harder challenges in one area, but they might have something else that's much better in return. Maybe I'm crazy, but knowing that helps.

I often worry that I haven't accomplished my dreams or reached my potential—like, say, some beautiful, ridiculously famous actor or singer. The amount of success these people have achieved is mind-boggling to me. Clearly, they'll never regret not fulfilling their potential, right? Or at least that's what it seems like from the outside. And yet—life is 50/50 for them, too. Even the rich and famous! What does that look like? I imagine they sometimes have to do things they don't enjoy. I can't imagine what it's like to have every little thing scrutinized, or not to be able to leave your house without swarms of fans following you. In their day-to-day lives, they might be just as happy—or unhappy—as anyone else. And that concept blows my mind.

I'm not saying all my ambition is gone. I still want to pursue my dreams, but knowing that I can be just as happy with or without the success takes the pressure off. You can pursue your passions and goals, knowing that you can be 100% as happy right now as you'll ever be. You get to choose to be as happy as possible *right now*.

Isn't that kind of amazing?

That brings me to my next lesson, something I learned both in coaching and from a manifestation coach I really enjoy, Juliet Cleary.

You Get to Decide

It was close to my birthday, and I told my life coach that what I really desired for my birthday was to have my ideal body. At that time, I followed a fitness influencer/instructor who I thought was the *sh*t*. It was 2020, and everything had just gone virtual, so I was doing a lot of online workouts from her. She was the creator of a dance fitness class called WERQ, which became my absolute favorite. To me, she had the "perfect" body: a small waist, almost no body fat, a rather juicy butt that she was incredible at shaking, and super toned arms and legs. Honestly, that sounds incredible to me now, too.

My coach responded, "You can have your ideal body right now. Decide that you are your ideal body." As you can imagine, that wasn't the answer I was looking for, and it certainly didn't satisfy me. I kind of rolled my eyes and started listing all the flaws I saw in my body.

She used this terminology repeatedly, and over time, it made more sense in different contexts. For a long time, my biggest hang-up had been my body, thanks to 90s and 2000s magazines and culture. So maybe that moment wasn't the best time for the lesson to sink in. But it made so much more sense as time went on.

"You get to decide" became a very meaningful and empowering phrase for me. You get to decide how you feel. You get to decide what to do. You get to decide what works for you and what doesn't. And most importantly, you get to decide who you *are*. You get to decide it all—you are not a passenger in your own life.

This idea was reinforced by the manifestation coach I follow on YouTube, Juliet Cleary.

I'll try to explain these ideas as clearly as I can.

You get to decide if you will be happy right now or not. It's an actual choice. Some people may naturally have a more positive outlook, and for others, it might be harder. But ultimately, it's a choice. You get to decide if holding a grudge is worth it or how to feel about your life and circumstances.

Sometimes, this is easier than at other times. There are moments when your body takes over, and you just feel horrible, and you need to process that emotion and let it go. (That'll be discussed in another chapter.) But at the end of the day, it's still true that you get to decide.

The number of things we unconsciously decide on every day is astounding. Our job is to bring some of these decisions to light. As Juliet Cleary teaches, you decide who you are every moment of your life. But most of these decisions are unconscious, shaped by your past. The amazing part is, you get to decide your future from a blank slate every single moment.

This may sound wild, but hear me out: you aren't taking your past with you. Your past does not define you, no matter how much you may want to believe that. So, when you go to interact with someone based on who you were in the past, you are, in fact, making a choice.

You might say it's ingrained and not a choice, but a habit. And that's true—it's a habit. But once you become aware of your habits, they're no longer unconscious, and that's when it becomes much easier to address them.

You may have a habit of always spiraling or getting upset in a particular situation. But so what? Is that a reason to keep doing it? Of course not.

You get to decide who you are in each moment. You could say, "I am currently the most self-confident version of myself." You can step into her, embody her, and be her in that moment. That's the decision. You can decide you are a mom who is very patient. You can pause for a moment and think, "How would the best version of myself handle this situation?" Would she scream and freak out? Or would she set firm boundaries and uphold them lovingly? Just having that plan is incredibly helpful. It's like preparing for a job interview—it gives you the confidence to step into the best version of yourself.

A good habit to form is to decide who you want to be and then ask yourself what that version of you would do before acting, instead of making decisions based on the past. That's old news— you get to be the new you right now.

Let's take a more obvious example. You need to interact with a person who is constantly rude to you. Every time you see them, you're acutely aware of this fact, and so, when you see them, you're already on guard, or you're rude back, or whatever the case may be. You're setting up the interaction for failure. You get to decide that this person likes you and then interact with them accordingly.

This doesn't mean you'll tolerate verbal abuse. But once again, you get to decide what you will and won't tolerate. You can be friendly and not care how they behave. If you have to see them every day, you can pretend they're nice (if you need to) and decide it's tolerable. Or, if it's not, you can decide to take a different course of action.

You could also decide to continue being passive-aggressive and complain to your friends and coworkers about this person. That's also a choice. And that's the point: it's all a choice. And when you step into that power, it feels damn good.

As it applies to motherhood, you get to decide a) what kind of mother you want to be and b) how you feel about your life.

Do you love your life? Do you love being a mother? Do you enjoy the good moments and breathe through the hard ones? Or do you resent the constant snotty noses and endless laundry?

As we discussed in the previous chapter, life is 50/50—full of both good and not-so-good moments—and that's normal. Maybe you're striving for something different, like more time for yourself, a better connection with your kids, or more patience, and that's great! But you get to decide to be happy right now, too.

I hope this is as exciting for you as it is for me because to me, it's empowering as hell.

I decided to be a calmer, more patient mother. It's as simple as that—a decision. It doesn't mean it always happens, but that decision means that everything I do comes from a place of knowing I made that choice. I can step into the calmest version of myself and see things from that perspective. And when I snap and lose my patience, I need to learn to soothe myself and recommit to the decision. But it all comes back to the decision. The highest version of myself wouldn't beat myself up for messing up.

I decide. I recommit. It's a simple formula.

Back to the body issues and deciding that my body is my ideal. I recently started working out at home again rather than at the gym. I put on this sports bra/crop top that I usually wear under a shirt and decided to just wear it with workout pants. I would never have been brave enough to wear that out in public at the time. But while I was working out like that, an unfamiliar feeling surged through me. I suddenly felt like that hot, fit chick you might see at the gym and envy. I felt strong, powerful, and…sexy. I was feeling myself. In that moment, I decided I *am* her. And I finally understood exactly what my life coach meant all those years ago (five years ago, to be exact). I felt it in my bones, and it felt so good.

"You get to decide" has become a mantra for me. I decided that I am rich, sexy, successful, an amazing mother—all the things.

Here's a wild story: I decided a while ago that my kids are really good. I started saying it so often that it became a natural thought (this is also called an affirmation, as mentioned previously). It's not that I didn't think my kids were great, but I didn't often think about them as just objectively good kids. I started saying it a lot because I was looking for an au pair and wanted to "sell" our family to them. But the more I said it, the more it became true. I started seeing them this way and treating them this way. And guess what? My kids are objectively great kids. That doesn't mean they never get on my nerves or that I'm never tired. It means I see the best in them most of the time.

The opposite is also true. Currently, I'm sad to say, I'm trying to organize my house. Not "reorganize" because it was never organized in the first place—just organize. Get a system in place. When I think about organizing, I get this panic response. My mind goes haywire, and I get overwhelmed by the thought (because it's the thought that's creating the feeling).

I had an organizer come recently to help me "learn" how to organize and put some sort of system in place. She came over for three hours. Those were some excruciatingly hard hours for me. At the end, I felt depleted. The organizer asked me, "What's stopping you from organizing? What are your main hurdles?" That conversation made me think. I realized I get overwhelmed just thinking about organizing. I remembered the times I sat in the play area reorganizing toys for hours, only to barely make a dent, and then have it all return to chaos a week later. As I said this, tears welled up in my eyes. I kept saying that I just lacked the organizational brain or skills I wished I had.

I said this because I believed it. I 100% believed I lacked organizational skills, and I kept saying it! Meanwhile, I recognize that our thoughts create our results. I complain about how much I hate organizing, and how bad I am at it, and how terrible it is.

How has this served me? What's the result? The result is that I've decided I'm a terrible organizer who hates organizing—and yet I yearn to live in an organized space. I've perpetuated this thought so deeply that it appears completely, objectively true. I've basically made a decision that goes completely against my desires.

So what would happen if I changed that to, "I am so good at organizing, and I love to organize!" as my primary thought? Just typing that makes me feel lighter and happier. I imagine myself happily organizing my home, having a place for everything, and finally living my dream minimalist, clutter-free lifestyle. Ahhh, a breath of fresh air!

This is my next challenge, clearly. I need to practice what I preach. I'm deciding, right now, as I type these words, to practice that new mantra on purpose. I am an organized person who happily organizes everything—damn it!

Update: I spent a week organizing things. It took all my energy, but suddenly, I had the "organization brain" I craved! I magically understood where to put things, what to throw out, what to donate, and what to label. That has never happened to me before. I assure you, this did not come naturally, but I did it. And you can, too!

It's not mystical, it's rational. My brain strove to prove me right, and look at that, it did!

Even more of an update: Because I took so long to finally release this book, a lot has changed. We bought a house (woohoo!) and got rid of a lot. I mean a lot. My goal was to get rid of at least 50% of our stuff and while that's actually difficult to measure, I think we were close to that goal or even surpassed it.

We moved into our new home, and I am so proud of the way my brain has started working. I have put thought into every detail. I have a color and style theme running throughout the home and if something doesn't have a place, then it isn't that needed. I have no design experience, but I will personally pimp myself out as THE up-and-coming designer to watch for (just kidding!). But that is a massive, and I mean massive change from when I originally wrote this book about 6 months prior. You never know where life will take you and once you start changing your beliefs, you have no idea who the new you will be. I do not recognize myself in relation to this in the best way and honestly, I'm pretty f*cking proud.

Be the Observer

I remember going to the bathroom and taking this idea of "being the observer" to the extreme. It felt like I was spying on myself, like a peeping Tom, and it was uncomfortable!

I don't think that's exactly what my coach meant by "being the observer."

I laughed about this with her when I mentioned it, but obviously, that's not what it means.

Being the observer is a way to put space between yourself and your overwhelming thoughts. It's the key to quieting a very loud mind that just won't leave you alone. I fall into this trap often and need reminders—just like with most other things in life.

When we have thoughts that feel overwhelming, we tend to get consumed by them. We're right in the middle of them, struggling to breathe. But to create space between you and your thoughts, you must—yep, you guessed it—be the observer. You start to step back, watch yourself, and observe your thoughts from a distance.

"I am feeling angry. I wish someone would try to understand me. I keep feeling like I'm not being heard."

It's like narrating your own life. By naming what you're feeling, it takes some of the sting out. It doesn't necessarily make everything go away, but it can turn down the intensity. This is especially helpful during moments of intense pain or rage.

Another way I'd describe it is like being in a pool of your own messy thoughts. You're drowning in them, but then, you climb out to the edge of the pool. You still see the thoughts swirling around, but you can breathe. You can relax for a moment.

Let's say you're getting worked up by a situation with your kids. It might go something like this:

"I'm feeling so frustrated. No one listens to me. We need to leave the house, and the kids are still just playing. I've given them a thousand warnings, and they're still not ready. I feel guilty for always being late, and now, here we are, late again. This makes me so angry."

Can you tell I'm very familiar with this situation?

By stepping into the observer role, you activate a more logical part of your brain. It's like watching a show. You may empathize with the characters, but you're not losing your mind over it. In the moment this is very hard to do, at first. I'm not saying any of this comes naturally—it won't. This isn't something we've been taught in school or that we saw our parents doing. It comes with practice, much like learning a new language. It feels awkward at first, but with time, it gets easier.

This technique is also useful when observing what your kids are doing, instead of, as my coach would say, "jumping into the pool with them." (Apparently, pool analogies are popular in this chapter.)

I've gotten significantly better over time with this concept. There was a period when my daughter would scream and freak out over everything. Her shoe would fall, and she'd scream. I'd dare go down the stairs without carrying her (even though I'd be right back up) and she'd yell. Really, anything and everything would set her off. It was exhausting. And I'd freak out right along with her. Her yelling triggered me, and I'd start melting down, too. And guess what? It made her more upset.

Something has shifted in the last few years. Now, when my kids scream, fight, or when my toddler has a meltdown, I'm usually able to be the calm, maybe slightly annoyed, observer. I watch, I show empathy, and I offer support—but I don't internally freak out like I used to. The internal dialogue might look something like this:

"He's screaming. He isn't hurt. He's really upset about something the other kids did. I'll offer him a hug. He's pushing me away and swatting at me. He's not ready for comfort yet. I'll check on him in a little bit."

And that's it. No drama from me. Yes, he's still freaking out, and it's loud, but I can step away from it and still be okay. I can still offer love and support without losing my sanity.

We all have an internal narrator. Your internal narrator doesn't have to freak out along with your thoughts. You don't have to panic just because your thoughts are spiraling. You can choose not to react.

Sometimes, our bodies feel overwhelmed, too. The feelings manifest in parts of our body—like tightness in your chest or muscles starting to stiffen. When I'm running late (which, let's face it, happens all the time), I feel like I'm crawling out of my skin. It's an incredibly unpleasant feeling. But you can observe this happening, too.

"My skin is tingling. I'm starting to panic. I can feel anger rising in my chest."

This is a way to get out of your head and reconnect with your body. It helps your body calm down faster.

As life lessons tend to do, they show up everywhere until you learn them and stop resisting. Here's another recent example. The other night, I had racing thoughts about something that made me question my skills—and deeper still, my self-worth. I woke up in the middle of the night, and when I have racing thoughts like that, it's tough to fall back asleep. But I remembered to be the observer and get out of the pool. I saw the mental chaos, but from a higher vantage point, not in the thick of it. That distance allowed me the space to relax enough to fall back asleep. I had spent the whole day crying and dealing with those emotions, so I'm not suggesting you push feelings away or stuff them down. But sometimes, we need a break from the noise, and being the observer allows us that luxury.

Notice in all these scenarios, we're not judging or pushing the thoughts away. We're simply observing what's happening. There's no need to label it as good or bad—it just *is*. This is an important point because judging and pushing away are the worst things we can do.

Judging yourself only adds to the pain. When you already feel the pain of a situation and then add in a dash of shame, it only makes things worse.

One of my life coaches taught me about the "shame sandwich." More on that later. But imagine this: You feel overwhelmed by your kids. Then, you judge yourself for feeling overwhelmed, thinking, "I should be enjoying every moment with them!" And then, to top it off, you throw in more shame for judging yourself: "Ugh, I know I'm not supposed to judge myself! I need to stop shaming myself!" And voilà! The perfect recipe for feeling like complete and utter crap.

Don't do that.

When I was in coaching, I felt immense judgment and shame for not understanding all the concepts right away. "Hello, I've been doing this for almost a year! Why do I keep needing coaching sessions and reminders?"

I wasn't being the observer—I was being the harshest judge. Obviously, that didn't help me learn or embrace the concepts. All it did was keep me in pain.

Imagine observing your friend and saying something like, "Wow, she's really losing her sh*t. What's wrong with her? Does she even know how to parent? Ooo, she's messing up her kids!" Would you say that to your friend? How would you feel if your friend said that about you? Would you still be friends after that?

And yet, we keep doing this to ourselves. It's not helpful. It'll keep you stuck. And it's going to cause unnecessary pain.

Let's talk a little bit more about pain. Shall we?

Feel Your Damn Feelings, Already

Have you ever seen a running river with a dam or rocks blocking its path? The fresh, clean water gets trapped, turning stagnant. Over time, it becomes muddy, smelly, and filled with bugs. While this may create a whole new ecosystem in real life, for this analogy, we'll ignore that and say it's a lot like your emotions when you try to push them down.

Stuck. Stagnant. And, with enough pressure, ready to burst.

I grew up living with my mom and stepdad. My mom was always emotionally unstable—easily triggered and upset. My stepdad, on the other hand, was less openly emotional. He seemed calm and wouldn't say anything was bothering him. Then, out of nowhere, something as insignificant as a tiny spill of tea would set him off. He'd lose it over something like that, start arguing, and tell you all the horrible things you'd done.

Neither of them was easy to live with. Over time, I realized my stepdad was like that river, blocking his emotions until they built up and overflowed. My mom, while more expressive, was also, in my unprofessional opinion, trying to push her emotions away. While I'm not a psychologist, I've tried to understand where my own patterns came from and why I behave the way I do. For many of us, our mothers are the first examples of how we're "supposed" to see and react to the world.

My mom was quick to be triggered, but she'd quickly blame others for setting her off. She was afraid of her emotions and wanted to hide from them. So, while her feelings did come out, they weren't really being felt or processed fully.

And here's the thing—I inherited that pattern. That's what I tend to do. Neither of these reactions is a winning situation.

You can't run from your feelings, but you can let them pass through you.

If blocking your feelings is like being the dam or the rock blocking the river, then feeling your feelings is like being a stone in the river that lets the water pass over it.

This doesn't come naturally to me—and I'm guessing it doesn't for most of us.

What I tend to do is "feel the feelings," then argue with them, explain them away, and judge them. Oh, the judging is real.

Feeling your feelings means that when emotions inevitably come (because, hey, we're all human), you don't do anything about them. They just come. Like a wave washing over you. (Yes, I realize I've used a lot of water analogies in this book, but bear with me.)

The feelings will pass. And they may come back again and again—it might take a few rounds. But the moment you start saying, "I shouldn't feel this way" or "What's wrong with me?" or "Why am I being so emotional?" you're arguing with your feelings and trying to push them away. And guess what? Your feelings always win.

According to Healthline.com:

"Everyone carries unprocessed emotions from experiences to some degree. However, emotions that aren't dealt with don't just go away. They can affect:

- The way you think about yourself

- How you react to stress

- Your physical well-being

- Your relationships with others"

There's a book called *The Body Keeps the Score*, which discusses this idea in depth. While many of us think of trauma as only being "serious"—like car accidents or violence—our minds can interpret so many things as trauma. One thing I learned from coaching is that more of us carry trauma than we realize because it can stem from the smallest things. We may not know exactly where it comes from, but I believe trauma comes from not fully processing situations and the emotions tied to them.

A few years ago, I had an incredibly painful situation with my mom. We were once very close, and I thought we always would be. I'm an only child, so I expected that relationship to remain strong. She was a big part of my kids' lives, too, before my third child was born. But a few years ago, things started to change. She actively started to push me away. I won't get into the whole story here, but suffice it to say, it hurt me deeply. Then, she moved from Chicago to Arizona, and I haven't seen her since (she came back once, but she was only here to see the kids, and we didn't talk much).

Obviously, this was a huge trauma for me. I don't understand it, and I may never understand it. My husband watched everything unfold and has no explanation other than, "It's like she went insane." For a long time, I was on the brink of tears every time I thought about it. I tried everything to fix the situation, cried about it countless times to my husband and life coach.

But the last time I spoke to my life coach about it, I said, "I don't understand why this keeps making me cry. I thought I had already accepted it. I already processed it. What the actual f*ck?"

I remember her response clearly: "Asya, the reason this keeps making you cry is because you keep asking, 'Why is it making you cry?'"

I had to let those words sink in. It was true. I didn't even realize I was doing that.

While I thought I was letting the feelings go, I was really just judging them and myself. And that's not how you process feelings.

After that conversation, I just cried—maybe even bawled. I let it all flow. I was taking a walk, crying, and letting all the hurt rush over me. And it sucked. But it was the last time I needed to do that. After years of trying to process, understand, and make sense of it, I finally just let it wash over me—no judgment, no pushing it away, just feeling.

That was the key, and I didn't even realize it. When we cry and think, "Okay, is this over yet?" we're trying so hard to run from the feeling or shrink from it. That's how we keep our feelings stuck.

If you want to let your feelings go, let them go. Don't hold on to them, don't judge them, don't stifle them. Let yourself cry. Let yourself scream. How long will it last? I have no idea. And that's okay. You don't need to know. What if it lasts a day? An hour? Who cares? The alternative is that it lasts years and then comes out at the most inappropriate time imaginable.

That said, there are times when your body and mind are completely overtaken by emotion, and you can no longer change your thoughts or simply let the feelings pass through. In those moments, you may need to soothe yourself. At that point, you're just taking care of yourself. You may need to ask, "What would feel the best for me right now?" Maybe it's getting a coffee, taking a walk, or watching a movie. Whatever it is that you can do reasonably in that moment, you need to do. This is the point where you can no longer "talk yourself out of your feelings." They may linger for a while, but we can still practice feeling them and not judging them, and we can soothe ourselves.

This is a good time to talk about presence. Being present—being fully in the moment—helps you connect with what feels good. There's a big difference between eating a cookie with a steaming cup of tea and really savoring the flavors, textures, and feelings of the cookie, versus scarfing it down because you feel you "deserve" it, while not really even tasting it. One comes from being grounded in the present moment, and the other is a distraction, a way to push feelings away, just like people drink to forget their problems.

Being present is about connecting to your body and how you feel right now. It helps move the feelings through your body. You can notice tension in your chest, or your neck and shoulders feeling stiff. Just that awareness can help alleviate some of the heaviness you may be feeling.

In the present moment, you can also really feel into what feels good as you soothe yourself. When you drink that cup of tea, feel the steam on your face, the warmth in your hands, and the smoothness on your tongue. Ground yourself in that moment, rather than trying to escape.

One way to help move the feelings along is to find a physical release for them. This could be an intense workout, where you focus entirely on the movement and forget about everything else (I love that!). Or, another technique I've heard of but have yet to try myself is a cold shower, a cold plunge, or putting your face in ice water for 15 seconds. If that sounds as unappealing to you as it does to me, then maybe you won't try it, and that's okay! But I can see how it might reset your body so you can move away from the feeling and move through it.

I used to take this really intense workout class at the gym, and after my first or second class, I told the teacher, "Your class is very relaxing!" I'm pretty sure she'd never heard that before. I explained that because the class was so intense and focused, I couldn't think about anything else, and it was great!

Journaling is another option I've recently discovered. Writing it all out helps—it's like having a conversation with yourself. If you want, you can even use an app like Otter.ai, which transcribes what you say. I often leave voice messages to a friend, but journaling is different. I end up having a full-on conversation with myself, rather than waiting for a friend's response. Sometimes, waiting for wisdom from others makes it worse because I expect something incredible, and when I don't get it, I don't know what to do. Journaling, though, is a way to answer my own questions.

Here's an example: Let's say you're having issues with your child not listening. If you walk through why that's so terrible, it might look something like this: "My kids don't listen because I'm a bad parent. Because they don't listen, they'll never be able to thrive. They won't get good jobs, and I'll have to support them forever—all because I'm a horrible parent!"

Now, is that true? No. Is it even logical? No. But it sure feels true in your brain! But once you write it out, you can see the irrationality of it. Then you can start questioning those thoughts. "Does my kid not listening to me today mean I'm a bad parent and they'll fail in life? No, probably not. This is a normal stage. I just need to find ways to connect with my child, and then listening will get easier."

That's how you find the solution you didn't even know was inside you. One thing I can promise you is that you can't solve the problem from the frantic energy that comes when those feelings first hit you.

While I can feel my feelings, sometimes they come back in waves when I think about what's bothering me. A new rush of pain can flood in. That usually happens when it's a fresh wound—when something just happened and my mind can't let it go. All I can do is soothe myself.

On that note...

It's Okay to Be Sad—That Goes for Both You and Your Kids

As I wrote this, it was my baby's third birthday! Woohoo! He's a cute, funny little guy (I call him "little baby") and just ridiculously adorable. Naturally, his birthday is all about him. But that concept can be hard for kids to grasp.

I have two other kids, at the time, they were 5 and 7. That day, while working, I told our au pair (in case you don't know, an au pair is like a live-in nanny) that they could take the kids to Kid's Empire, a play place they usually beg to go to. It's expensive, so I don't take them there every week, but for a birthday, we're pulling out the big guns!

But my 7-year-old didn't want to go. I asked him why, and although he couldn't fully express his feelings, it became clear: he didn't like that his brother was the one deciding what they were doing. Normally, he'd love to go to Kid's Empire, but that day, he didn't want to go because *his brother* was making the decision, not him. It seemed like a mix of jealousy and not wanting to be told what to do.

So, what do I do as a parent? Do I give in to his wishes and do everything I can to make sure he doesn't feel bad? Do I restructure the whole day to make him happy and avoid any bad feelings?

No. Absolutely not. That sounds insane. Nobody would recommend doing that. And honestly, many would say this is a crucial lesson for a 7-year-old: sometimes, it's not about what you want. Sometimes, we have to do what someone else wants—not just what we want. So often, as parents, we give up our own desires to please our kids. Here, for one day, he gets to experience what it feels like when someone else makes the call.

These are all great lessons.

But there's another lesson here that adults often don't learn.

He feels bad about something. And that's okay.

But as adults, what do we do when we feel bad? We run. We hide. We numb the feeling. We do anything to forget it. We can't bear to feel bad. And all of that stems from childhood.

You know when parents are really quick to tell kids, "You're okay" and try to cheer them up in every way possible? That makes us afraid of our feelings. Or when parents scold their kids for feeling a certain way? That's also not helpful because it teaches kids to push their feelings away. But then, they feel shame for having those feelings while still being forced to deal with them.

So, do yourself and your child a favor: don't do any of that.

I hugged my 7-year-old and told him, "I know this is hard, but this is how it works on people's birthdays. He gets to decide what we do on his birthday, just like you got to decide on yours, and your sister got to decide on hers."

He didn't feel better immediately, but he agreed to go. He didn't have much else to say about it. He just needed his feelings to be heard and validated. And really, isn't that what we all need?

I've mentioned this before, but it can be hard in the moment and it's worth repeating. I sometimes have dark moods that I can't shake, and I just want to feel better. But the harder I try to make it go away, the worse it gets. Instead, we can just be still and let it be. We can recognize that it's okay to feel sad or upset, even if we don't fully understand why. The more we try to run from it, the worse off we are. And don't get me started on when we then judge ourselves for having the bad feelings, because that judgment brings in shame. I've spoken about this shame sandwich before—it's not helpful.

There's a saying: "It's okay not to feel okay." And that's exactly what I'm getting at here. But I want to add one more line: *it's also okay to feel okay*. Sometimes, it's hard to let go of a bad mood and enjoy good moments because we think we need to resolve the bad mood first. Maybe it's a sense of "gatekeeping" our feelings, where we think we must control them. I'm not sure. But that's why I want to add: it's okay not to feel okay, AND it's okay to feel okay, even in the middle of not feeling okay.

We're parenting our kids, but many of us need to reparent ourselves. We need to understand that there's nothing to be ashamed of and nothing to run from. These life lessons only become clear when we let them be. Just like we can't scramble to make our kids' hard feelings go away, we can't do that for ourselves and expect a good outcome.

We sit. We feel. And then we move through them.

Move Through the Sh*tty Feelings

Netflix binges are amazing. Ice cream is delicious. Retail therapy is divine. But feeling like crap and trying to outrun your feelings? That's horrible, and nobody wants that.

Listen, I love a good Netflix binge as much as the next person. I will never take that away from you (never!). They're a necessity in life. But there's a difference between saying, "I finally get to watch my favorite show after a long day and relax!" and "I feel like crap, I want to cry, so let's turn on a show." The same goes for ice cream or shopping.

Do a vibe check. Where is it coming from? Is it excitement or desperation? Is it a way to soothe yourself or a way to outrun feelings you don't want to feel?

The other week, I had a rough week. One thing I noticed is that when I fall into the deep depths of despair, it usually happens when I haven't gotten enough sleep or rest, or when something else has thrown me off balance, making me super susceptible to it. At that point, all the coaching techniques in the world can't seem to save me.

Obviously, if you can prevent that from happening, do so. But sometimes it's unavoidable. And then, when it hits, the only option is to move through the feelings.

How do you do that? You've got to move it, shake it, and get those feelings out of your body!

Part of the process is sitting with the discomfort and really letting the feeling wash over you, as we just discussed. But sometimes, that's not enough—at least, not for me. Sometimes I do let the feeling wash over me, and it goes away. But then it comes back or completely takes over my body, and I just feel bad again.

It feels horrible, but I know that pushing those feelings away definitely won't help.

Here are some ideas to help you get those mother f*cking feelings out! Once they're out, you can come up with a solution from a calm and productive place. This isn't about outrunning your feelings; it's about moving through them so you can shift to a more solution-focused, productive state. Do one of these, do all of these, or do whatever feels right. The point is to move the feelings out.

Journaling:
I used to dismiss journaling because it didn't work for me. I didn't understand the point, and my hand would get tired trying to write as fast as my thoughts. But this past summer, I tried it again, and somehow, it was different. It helped me turn around my thoughts and stop running them in circles in my mind. Try it out and see if it helps. There may be times when it works and times when it doesn't, but it's always available and within reach.

Dance, Move, Punch:

People often recommend going for a walk to clear your mind. For me, a walk is mindless enough to allow my thoughts to take over, so it doesn't help. But dancing or moving in a more engaging way helps move that energy and occupies your mind. I'm sure I don't have to tell you how helpful punching can be when you're angry. Cardio kickboxing is great because you follow the choreography while getting to punch and kick the emotions out. I personally take karate, and I love punching, kicking, and yelling with full force.

Extreme Sensations:

Running your hands under cold water, holding a hot cup of tea, or putting your face in ice water are all examples of how you can reconnect with your body and break free from your mind's circus. These physical sensations ground you in the present moment and help you move the energy instead of letting your thoughts spiral. Obviously, don't hurt yourself, but you can do something that shocks your system and helps you reconnect with your body.

Finding Something Funny:

This may involve a show or two, but I recommend a comedy or sitcom. Laughing can completely shift your mental state and put you in a better place once you're ready for it. Again, not to distract, but to *move* through them.

Talk It Out:

This is similar to journaling but may work better for some. You can record yourself talking into an app like Otter.ai, which transcribes what you say, so you can look over it and get new ideas. You could also voice message a friend, which is a great option, but I like the idea of discussing the issue with yourself. It's empowering and can be done anytime, anywhere. Often, when we get the problem out—on paper or in a recording—we can put some space between it and ourselves. That's helpful. Another tool I've been using is ChatGPT, which is free AI. Think whatever you want of AI, but put to good use, it can be life changing. You go to chatgpt.com, put your thoughts in, and it can reflect to you what you're thinking, what your main pain point is, go through it with you, whatever you want. For me, it's been a game changer.

Meditate:
I don't always connect with meditation, but it's incredibly helpful for many. You can find a specific meditation for stress or anxiety on YouTube to target what you're feeling, rather than a meditation on money or something unrelated to the moment.

Find What Excites You the Most:
Bashar, a spiritual leader well-known in the manifestation community, has a concept called the "Follow Your Excitement Formula." I'll write more about this later, but for now, I'll summarize it briefly: The idea is to find what excites you the most in any given situation and follow that excitement. It might be getting a fancy coffee from a cafe, taking a walk, going to the store, putting on music, or baking a cake. Ask yourself what feels most exciting and possible at that moment, and go with it. Lately, I've been asking myself this a lot.

Scream into a Pillow:
Sometimes, it just feels good to scream or knock things over.

Since we don't want to worry our neighbors, I recommend muffling the sound with a pillow. Or, throw around a pillow or some stuffed animals. Sometimes, you just need a safe way to get that aggression out.

Music:

Music can be a game changer. If you have a go-to artist or song, have it ready for those times when you need a lift. Music can pivot your mood on the spot. You probably already know the kind of music that makes you smile, so start gathering ideas for what you can listen to when you need it most. Personally, I've been getting into playing music on my Ukulele—it makes me smile. I love practicing, learning new songs, and hearing it all come together.

Once you've done one (or more) of these and you're feeling better, you can tackle the problem that set you off in the first place and figure out a game plan.

One thing that really aggravates me is feeling powerless in situations involving my kids when they don't listen. For example, if I ask them to clean up their room or leave the park and they don't listen, it leaves me feeling out of control. So, I need to come up with a plan for what to do next time it happens so that I'm prepared. But I know that in the moment of anger, I can't do anything to fix the problem.

To recap: Once we've processed our feelings, we want to get them out somehow (and continue to process them if needed). We want to change our state of mind and get out of our heads and into our bodies. Then, we can regroup and come up with an actual solution for next time.

Support Your Body as Well as Your Mind

I've been writing about mindset for a while now, and I will always swear by it as a key element of success in life. But...let's talk about something that needs attention:

Your body chemistry.

I'm all about changing your thoughts, feeling amazing because of it, and really working on a fresh perspective. But here's the truth—I've learned that you cannot ignore your body.

As I've mentioned before, I always wanted three kids, and guess what? I got three kids—yay! But, when I wasn't getting a full night of sleep, I hated having any kids, let alone three. I tried very hard to power through, to be okay. Sometimes, I even succeeded. I worked out, talked to my life coach regularly, tried changing my thoughts and perspective, etc. But guess what I *really* needed? Sleep. Rest. Time to just be. And probably magnesium and vitamin D, and who knows what else.

For all that time, I was only focusing on my mind, and let me tell you—it was an uphill battle. Sure, you can do a lot with your mind, and that's been my premise for years. But it's 1,000% harder if you aren't supporting your body.

I've definitely fallen victim to forgetting that sometimes, my body needs care: relaxation, supplements, sleep, time to unwind, etc.

These days, even though I get more sleep than I did a year ago, I still need time to unwind. I'm a huge fan of exercise and walks, and I make time for them every day. But I also need time to be lazy, watch a show, play the ukulele (my instrument of choice), and just be.

Note: Just to clarify, I am very much against the generic advice of "just take a walk" to feel better. It's basic at best, and harmful at worst. Sure, it's necessary to incorporate mindset tools, but otherwise, a walk, massage, or whatever else you're told is often just a time to ruminate and spin your wheels—definitely not enough on its own.

The other piece of this is allowing yourself to relax and take care of the person who matters most: YOU. We are humans, and our needs change from day to day and differ from everyone else's. I'm a very emotional person, and let me tell you, it's exhausting. I often feel like I don't have a "right" to feel tired because I have the privilege of doing more things for myself than many others.

Whether that's true or not is irrelevant. I need what I need. I don't need to justify it. I just know it—and when I don't get it, I feel like crap.

Last week, I reorganized all the kids' toys in the playroom and their bedroom. I took everything out—threw away the junk, donated what they hadn't played with, and put everything back in its place, organized by category and labeled. I also cleaned up the backyard, tossing out all the broken toys and anything too weathered to use anymore. This took *everything* out of me. I mean, everything. To someone else, this may feel energizing. For me, it's incredibly draining (but necessary, which is why I did it). I wasn't in a good mood afterward. I felt the need to explain this to myself and my kids, but looking at it in writing, it seems obvious: I had nothing left to give to anyone else. As the saying goes, *you can't pour from an empty cup*.

My biggest downfall, and I'm sharing this because I'm sure I'm not the only one, is the need to justify all of this to myself. But I don't need to. My brain needs reminding that I don't need to feel guilty. I don't need to feel bad. I don't need to justify.

And neither do you.

If you snap, and all your mindset techniques aren't working, it's not because you failed. It's because you need something more.

How do you figure out what you need? Trial and error. Right now, I'm trying magnesium cream. It's supposed to help with relaxation, and I think I've noticed a difference. I probably need more things to support relaxation, and I'll be doing more research on it. I don't know what *you* need, but I do know this: If your mindset journey feels impossible or isn't working, you might need some body chemistry support. And that's a great place to start!

I should also note that as parents, it's not always possible to get what we need. We have a lot on our plates. We do what we can with what we have. I know sleep isn't always possible for parents of young kids. And yes, that's torture. I know. But we *can* make it a priority to get whatever rest and support we can. Maybe that means getting a babysitter to sleep. If you feel that's too expensive or luxurious, then try swapping babysitting duties with a friend or acquaintance with kids. You can get creative when you put your own rest and needs first. If you declare that you will get the support you need—and mean it—your mind will find a way. You'll come up with new ideas or opportunities you never thought of. But you have to recognize how important it is for you and make it a priority. When people say, "Make time," that's what they mean. If you declare it, you'll figure it out, I promise.

Presence and Neutrality Beat "Hard Work"

Yes, this may sound weird. I know. This chapter was the hardest for me to write because I'm not entirely sure how to clarify what I mean, but here we go.

I've always worked hard and done all the "right" things in life. I think many of us have. There's a certain route we're told to take, sold as the promise to success.

I went to school, got straight A's, took all the AP classes, went to a "good" university, etc. I went to grad school, got married, had kids, blah, blah, blah. I love my husband. I love my kids. But despite all of that, I often felt deeply unfulfilled and, quite frankly, annoyed.

I worked so hard to do all these things, but it's not that I didn't want to do them or thought they were bad. It's that they never brought me any *real* joy. The goalposts kept moving. You finish one thing, and then you're on to the next, never really finding a moment to stop and enjoy it.

As much as I want to enjoy life, more than anything, I want to be happy. And you know what? Very few people actually are.

Most people I know are married, have kids, jobs, live in a good area, all that jazz. But what unites everyone? What do they all love to do? Complain. They love to complain.

I don't think this is helpful. I find it unproductive (I'm not talking about the initial venting of a situation where you want a different perspective—that's helpful), and I have no desire to settle for it. Do you?

So, I want to try something different. That's what this entire book and journey are about.

I'm not saying hard work is bad. But I do think we need a different approach. If anything, we're often afraid of being "lazy," so we keep pushing ourselves without knowing when to stop.

Here's my theory: Relaxation and neutrality are the keys to success. I think we all need to try less. Certainly with less urgency. And for sure with less stress. I do NOT believe that "hard work" is what will get you far. We all work hard, especially as moms.

But are we happy? Has it gotten us to where we want to be? Maybe, in some ways, yes. It has brought us to certain things we appreciate and cherish. But on a smaller scale, zoomed in on the moment-to-moment, most people are not feeling all that great, at least, not as much as they could be.

We're too old for that. We can't sleep, we're constantly worried, money is draining, gas prices are up, we can't afford things, etc.

This is typical "adult" talk. Our happiness becomes completely dependent on what happens to us and the world around us. There will always be something to complain about, so we know this is not the best approach.

What if we ignored outside circumstances and focused on what's within ourselves? What if we pursued what we felt called to do, to the best of our abilities, and trusted ourselves to make the right decisions? Yes, sometimes we have to do things we don't necessarily want to do, but we can still relax into the moment and release the resistance we hold onto so tightly. We can still find enjoyment.

What do you think will happen?

I think you'll feel energized and restored, and everyone in your family and in your presence will feel it.

We are constantly trying to control everything, but the result is that we end up controlling nothing. We're so resistant to what is that we end up constantly fighting ourselves and reality. We feel like there's no way out because our resistance blocks us from having any good ideas.

In my opinion, the key is completely counterintuitive.

We need to accept what is around us in a more neutral state. All we need is to look around, see that it's there, and be the observer (all these concepts are connected). We need to put space between ourselves and the negativity we feel about the situation.

Every time we talk about our horrible circumstances, complain about how difficult things are, or look for advice from other struggling moms, we're just confirming to our minds that we hate our lives.

Even if you don't have any big "life problems," I'm willing to bet you're not feeling incredible from moment to moment. And if you are, well, go ahead and ignore me.

The key is to relax in the moment.

I don't mean go to the spa or get a pedicure. Not all of us can do that, especially when we have kids and no family around. I hate that kind of "advice." While it's lovely to get a pedicure, it doesn't make up for all the time we spend *not* taking care of ourselves. And, let's be real, it's simply not realistic for everyone. I'm talking about relaxing in the moment—even in the most stressful moments. Breathe into it and accept it. Stop narrating it negatively.

What we're doing when we hate something and wish it were different, or feel how unfair it is, etc., is resisting. And resisting is a big enough topic to merit its own chapter (coming soon to this book near you).

I believe resistance is the antithesis of happiness.

The first step is neutrality. Not assigning so much meaning to the things happening around us that we can't control. When we label things as "bad," we inherently make them hurt more. For example, if your child is crying and overwhelmed, calling it "bad" behavior makes it feel so much worse for you. But if you approach it for what it is—just a child crying—you can see more clearly what needs to be done. Your child probably needs a hug, rather than reacting from a triggered place of, "Oh my god, stop crying already!" and yelling.

A relaxed state of mind is more important than any pedicure you'll ever get. Time away from the kids is essential, and everyone knows that. But I'm not talking about the usual band-aid solutions. I'm talking about a totally different approach.

And I'm not saying just try, try, try to push through it. I've tried for a long time, and I can't do it anymore. We need to stop resisting. What if we took that energy and put it into the present moment instead?

This chapter ties in with other concepts like "being the observer" and "releasing resistance," and I debated whether it needs its own chapter. But that's what happens when you try to organize overlapping ideas into neatly laid-out chapters.

Neutralizing what happens helps us relax into the present moment. It's very similar to observing the moment. The key is to describe what's happening around you and inside you without assigning meaning to it.

It would look something like this:

"Oh look, no one did the laundry, and there's so much of it. I'm so annoyed. I have thought this thought many times. I have lots of complaints about this situation. I'm having thoughts about how I'm the only one doing laundry."

This observation takes the sting out of these thoughts. Then, we have space. Space feels amazing. Space allows new ideas and solutions to come in. When we're removed from the problem, we can see it with a fresh perspective. You don't get that by working harder—you can't force a new perspective.

In this particular scenario, you might come up with a new solution, like a laundry system where everyone is responsible for their own laundry, or they have no clothes. You might even discover that doing laundry is a moment to listen to your favorite audiobook while folding clothes, finding hidden joys that you couldn't see before because you were too busy hating it.

Another benefit of being a neutral observer is that you create room to feel good. Have you ever felt like you're not "allowed" to feel good until every problem is solved? But in this present moment, right here and now, you don't really have the problems you think you have.

All of our problems exist in the past or future. Right now, in this moment, you can breathe.

For me, what usually happens is I breathe in deeply and realize I've been holding a ton of tension in my shoulders (hello, tension headaches). As that tension releases, it feels really good. That moment is not the problem—the problem is me thinking about everything I need to fix.

Let's say you do have a problem right now that needs fixing. My "work harder" mindset kicks in, and I feel like I need to freak out and yell to fix it. Let's say the kids are fighting. Maybe they're yelling, screaming, and even hitting each other. My go-to response is, "This is so hard! I need to yell more and push them away from each other!"

Spoiler alert: That doesn't usually work. And if it does, it leaves me completely depleted. But if I were to be present, observing the situation with more neutrality, I could stay calm and find a solution much quicker—and much more quietly.

The energy of "hard work" is about pushing, shoving, yelling, and fixing. The energy of a neutral, relaxed mind is about saying, "Okay, I see this. This is what I will do."

This is a combination of relaxing into the moment, releasing resistance, being present, and being neutral. Let's talk a bit more about the pesky resistance I seem to love so much.

Release the Resistance

We were taking a trip with my mom and stepdad. It was me, my husband, my mom, my stepdad, our toddler, and our almost newborn baby, just a few months old. My husband was driving with my stepdad in the front, my mom and toddler were in the second row singing songs and having fun, and I was in the third row with a very unhappy, screaming baby.

I was pissed.

I mean really, how is that fair? The baby wouldn't sleep, and she hated every second of the hours-long car ride. It was horrible.

I immediately wrote to my life coach and told her what was going on. She said, "Asya, you're in resistance."

We'd talked about this many times, so I immediately understood what she meant. I let go of the resistance and felt better.

Nothing on the outside changed. The baby was still crying, and everyone else was still enjoying themselves. But I had let go of the tension and resistance I was holding on to.

The thing about resistance is that it's a sneaky little b*tch. You really don't know it's there unless you're very aware of yourself and your thoughts. I still need reminders sometimes, but I can tell you—it's more than worth it to learn how to let go of resistance.

So, what is resistance? It's that feeling of pushing against what's happening. It's when we think, "This shouldn't be happening! It should be different!"

It's the opposite of acceptance, and it causes a lot of pain.

I often experience a feeling of fear that if I release resistance, I'm "allowing" something I don't want to happen. But here's the thing: it was never mine to allow or not; I just thought it was.

We think we have control over everything, and in that illusion, we lose control of our own minds and feelings.

This may be one of the hardest and most important things to do. It's truly a practice that will take time. But if you remember nothing else from this book, remember that releasing resistance is key.

Have you ever decided to actively release tension and noticed your shoulders suddenly drop? That, in my opinion, is the resistance we're holding onto—it's like we won't allow ourselves to let go. And it serves no purpose!

F*ck the resistance!

Sometimes, I catch myself resisting thoughts as well. There's a very wise saying: "What you resist, persists." And it's true! The famous example is telling someone not to think of a pink elephant. Obviously, the first thing they'll think of is a pink elephant. Similarly, we have to let our thoughts just pass through us. The thought is there, and it just *is*. Let it be there rather than trying to fight it.

This may seem at odds with what I said earlier about how our thoughts create our results. And in some ways, it is. But sometimes, a thought is so persistent, we can't do anything about it. It's just there, lurking. Sometimes, it keeps you up at night. Sadly, this happens to me. I get intrusive thoughts in the middle of the night, and I can't go back to sleep. I lie there, trying to relax, but my mind just won't let me.

In the past, I would fight it, thinking about how important it is to sleep, trying to imagine a beach or some other relaxing place. I'm not saying that's bad, and if it works for you, mazal tov! But it never worked for me and just made me feel more anxious. Now, I just let the thoughts be. I try to relax as much as possible, knowing that this thought really needs to play out in my mind. I don't chase it with follow-up thoughts or go down a rabbit hole. I just let it be there.

Since I'm sure I'm not the only one who's been woken up by anxious thoughts, let's walk through an example:

You wake up to go to the bathroom, and when you get back into bed, your mind is wide awake, focusing on some problem you can't fix right now. "Oh no, I have so much to do before our vacation!" For that, you could get up and make a list to calm your mind. But what if it's something more pervasive?

"Why did I spend so much money on X? Was my haircut a huge mistake? Why did that woman call me 'ma'am'? I used to always be called 'miss,' I'm getting old, what should I do?"

Don't judge me—we've all been there.

So, you're lying awake with one of these thoughts. There's nothing you can do about it. You try to picture a beach or take deep breaths, but it's not working. Your mind is just racing. What can you do in that moment?

Lean into it. Say to yourself, "Okay, you won't settle down, I see that," and accept it. Accept that this won't be your best night of sleep. Accept that you have racing thoughts and they won't go away. At the very least, you can try to relax your body and release the physical tension. Relax into the thoughts—even the horrible ones. They're there to stay for the moment.

What you don't want to do is start adding to it, like, "He called me 'ma'am,' so I must look old, I must be ugly, I must be worthless!" (It's unfortunate, but these are often the messages we get from society.)

You can breathe into the feelings and thoughts rather than trying to escape them. I've found this works with pain too. Often, when I have a headache, I feel like I'm trying to run away from the pain in my body. But, of course, that doesn't work. It's the same with thoughts—trying to escape them won't help. If you don't believe me, try it and then come back and read the rest of this chapter.

Instead, breathe into them. Let them be there. Give them space without trying to confirm or deny them. Let's say the thought is, "I got a really bad haircut, it was a huge mistake." You think that thought and feel a sting of pain washing over you.

Let it.

That's it. Don't argue with it. "No, it'll grow back, it'll be okay! Maybe it isn't that bad. Oh god, why did the hairstylist let me do this to myself? That b*tch!"

Instead, just let it be there.

Yeah, you heard me. Let it be there. Don't engage. Don't attach. Don't push against it. Let it be. That's it.

That's when the resistance melts away, and the thought will eventually fade. It's so simple. How come no one ever taught us this?

You can certainly argue with this, like I did. You can ask, "What are your credentials? Who are you to tell me what to do? What do you know anyway?"

That's all fine—I understand. Don't believe me. Just try it. It's free!

Boundaries Aren't Selfish

As I was writing this, my kids came in and jumped all over me and the room I'm working in. So, I'm no expert on boundaries. I'm still working on it. But here's what I do know...

During one of my most recent calls with my life coach, I was in tears. It was all too much. I had been working at this one speech therapy clinic online (I'm a speech therapist) for a few years. When I decided to homeschool my kids, I asked them to change my schedule so I could work a few evenings a week. This didn't sound terrible at the time, but what happened was that I'd spend several intense hours with my kids doing all the mom things, and then, just when I would have given anything to take a break, watch a show, or enjoy a hobby, I'd have to go work for a few hours. Needless to say, that kind of sucked.

Then, I decided to take a new job for extra hours during the first half of the day.

On top of all that, my kids were in a theater program with a really terrible director/owner who seemed to verbally bully the kids, and they didn't want to go anymore. I had numerous calls with her, trying to explain how not to treat my kids.

I'm sure there were other things going on as well, but the point is: I was about to explode. My coach said, "Something has to go," and, of course, she was right. But what? I couldn't imagine what I could possibly get rid of. She asked me, "What would you cut out in your ideal world?" I had been wanting so badly to cut out my evening job, but that didn't seem possible for some reason. However, when I thought about it, it made me so happy! The idea of finally not working evenings sounded amazing.

I knew immediately what I needed to do, but I hadn't had the courage to do it. A few hours later, I told the owner, crying, because it's a really great clinic, that I couldn't do it anymore. Luckily, I was able to continue working there but with fewer clients. I decided to keep the two who stimulated me the most.

The reason I hadn't done this earlier was simple: guilt. Guilt got in the way. I didn't want to let the clinic down, I didn't want to let the clients down, and I didn't want to let my family down because it was good money. But ultimately, as I'm sure you can guess, who did I let down? Me. Obviously.

But that's how it often is with boundaries. We think we're being selfish by setting them, but in reality, we need them to keep our sanity.

Guilt is a strong motivator for me, unfortunately, and I find that it is for many people pleasers. We don't want to let others down, so we choose to let ourselves down instead. I'm this way as a boss too. I need to remind myself that my priority isn't for everyone to like me. I emphasize being respectful and kind, but sometimes, I let people take advantage of that. Being firm about boundaries is uncomfortable for me. But so what? We have to do uncomfortable things in life to grow, right?

I once lost it with my kids because, although we have an au pair (and I'm very grateful for that help), my kids would often see me as always "open for business." The au pair has strictly set hours, and the program is federal, so there are very specific rules on what's allowed. When he was off, he was off. But when I was "off" (is a mother ever really "off"?), aka working, they would still feel free to waltz in, even if I was talking to a client or writing notes (I work from home).

Knowing that a parent's job is 24/7, we *also* need time to relax, and my husband and I need time to go out together. But my kids had no regard for that.

The result? An overstressed mom who literally never got a break. I recognize that this might be a reality for many moms, and maybe I'm high-needs, but I really need a breather to keep my sanity. So, I needed to set a boundary. With the kids and with the au pair.

I have the disease of needing to please others—it's a bad case. I didn't even want to upset the au pair. You know, the person we pay to help with our kids? So, I bucked up and went to talk to him (we have a guy au pair, colloquially known as a "Bro pair").

I told him that when the kids are supposed to be with him, they must be with him. They can't come in and out of my office while I'm working or if I'm doing something. He said he wasn't sure what to do when they cry. I said that they'll need to get used to it, and it has to become the norm.

I felt so good after this talk, but believe it or not, it was very difficult for me! I know many will wonder why that would be difficult for someone, but that's who I am—a people pleaser in recovery.

These boundaries around our time and space are beyond necessary. And yet, if you're anything like me, and I know I'm not alone, it can be difficult not to be consumed by guilt. Usually, for moms, it's the guilt of not being with the kids enough or not working enough. We can't win.

But you can also create boundaries around your thoughts and decisions. Whatever decision you made is the right one. *The f*cking end*. And this is the best kind of boundary, I think.

Have you ever had a recurring thought that grabbed hold of you and wouldn't let you go? Maybe a doubt, a fear, a regret? "I should have never done X or Y, why didn't I just do Z instead?"

I learned that you have the power to yell, "STOP!!!" to those thoughts. And while that sounds easier said than done, it's actually kind of simple. This is one of the easiest things you can do for unhelpful thoughts.

I'll preface this by saying I'm an overthinker. I often have the same unhelpful thoughts about people judging me, worrying if I hurt someone's feelings, wondering if I'm good enough, etc. I'm very familiar with intrusive thoughts. So hear me out.

Just recently (a few days before writing this), I couldn't sleep. I had a thought that I can now admit to because it worked out okay. I had just gotten my third (and probably final) tattoo. I've always wanted a tattoo, my whole life! It took me 38 years to get my first one. I found an artist I liked and got my first one in May of 2024. I loved it so much that I quickly decided to get a second. It's gorgeous, with my kids' names on it. When I got the second, I looked in the mirror and thought, "There's something missing here," and pointed to my left collarbone. Almost immediately, I booked another appointment. I knew exactly what I wanted—a mountain design with the word "decide" written into it (see the chapter on decisions for why). But when I got the tattoo, which was gorgeous, I suddenly felt like all three tattoos were too much, and I made a huge mistake. It felt like the wrong placement, too close to the first tattoo on my left bicep. Now what?

I decided on the spot, no, this is not the case. Everything is perfect. I breathed into that thought. It didn't fully go away, but I acknowledged it and didn't let my mind wander further. Eventually, I fell back asleep without realizing it. When I woke up and remembered my worries, I said, "No, we're done here, and everything is perfect." I decided not to engage with that unhelpful thought. I didn't even mention it to my husband because I decided the thought was done.

Thankfully, this story has a happy ending.

The tattoo artist I go to uses a clear wrap called *Second Skin*. It was considerably bigger than the tattoo itself, and while it was clear, I didn't realize it made the tattoo look bigger and bulkier. When I took it off, I felt a huge sigh of relief—it looked so much better! Phew! That would've sucked.

Hopefully, you didn't get anything permanent done to your body that you deeply regret. But since pesky thoughts aren't just about tattoos, it's safe to say you know exactly what I'm talking about.

This was a case of a thought that wasn't helpful. Many of our thoughts are exactly that. They gnaw at you, drive you insane, and you can simply shut them down.

You don't want to resist the thought and push it away, because as I've said before, what we resist persists. But it's like telling an annoying companion to stop talking because you have a headache. The companion may start again, but you just politely say, "Thank you, we're done here."

I believe the key is a very easy attitude towards this. I've certainly had times where I tried to shut down thoughts forcefully, and that didn't work. That just creates more resistance and tension. But when it's done in a nonchalant way, I find it to be *easy*—and that's not something I typically experience with other techniques. This might be unique to me, though. Maybe you'll find other techniques here easy and this one hard. You won't know until you try!

As a little sidenote, I decided to shut down the guilt. I put up a hard thought boundary about it. If I am not with the kids, that's the right thing to do. If I am with the kids, guess what? That's also correct. Whatever I decide to do is the correct answer and that's all there is to it. Same goes for you, friend.

The "Bashar Lifestyle"

This is a new concept for me, one I recently learned about from the spiritual leader and guru, Bashar. He calls it "the formula," but I thought "The Bashar Lifestyle" sounded like a fun title!

According to his website, Bashar.org:

"Bashar is a physical E.T., a friend from the future who has spoken for the past 40 years through channel Darryl Anka. He has brought through a wave of new information that clearly explains in detail how the universe works, and how each person creates the reality they experience. Over the years, thousands of individuals have had the opportunity to apply these principles and see that they really work to change their lives and create the reality that they desire."

I don't know about the "physical E.T." part, but his teachings are really interesting. You can find more on his website or by searching for "Bashar" on YouTube—there are tons of videos and shorts of his teachings. That's how I discovered him.

From Bashar.org, here's his formula:

Step 1

Act on your excitement, your passion, whatever is most exciting to you in the moment. Do this every moment that you can.

Step 2

Do this to the best of your ability. Take it as far as you can until you can't take it any further.

Step 3

Act on your excitement/passion with absolutely no insistence, assumption, or expectation of what the outcome should be.

Step 4

Choose to remain in a positive state regardless of what happens.

Step 5

Constantly investigate your belief systems. Release and replace the unpreferred beliefs—fear-based beliefs, and those not in alignment with who you prefer to be.

I've been part of the manifestation community for quite a while now, but I often "fall off the wagon," letting negativity drag me down. I constantly feel like I haven't done enough, that I need to do more, that I'm not successful enough, or good enough—classic negative manifestation!

I had heard about this formula from Bashar before, but then another manifestation YouTuber, Rita Kaminski, mentioned that this formula changed her life. She gave an example that really illustrated how the formula worked for her. At first, she did small things, like watching a show. But then she got bored with it, started watching fitness content, and eventually began working out.

I thought that was such an interesting chain of events, because it shows how we never know where our excitement will take us.

I translated this to mean: do what feels best in the moment. I started asking myself, "What would make this moment feel better?" As parents, of course, we can't follow our excitement all the time (or even most of the time). Our weekends and evenings are often filled with our children's desires, and that can be draining. But what if we started asking ourselves, "How could I make this moment feel better?" What would change?

Bashar states in several videos that this is all you need. Just this. Simple. Pure. I'm not going to pretend that I completely understand it yet, but I can see how this shift in mindset can really change your approach to things.

As a parent, here's how I think this is helpful:

- You're heading somewhere for your kids, you're tired and don't want to go. What would help you feel better? Turning on your favorite music? Getting your favorite drink to go?

- You're cleaning up after dinner, and nobody took their plates off the table, there are crumbs everywhere, and you need to put the dishes away. Maybe you could turn on a YouTube video or listen to an audiobook while cleaning up?

- Your kids are fighting, and no one is listening. Maybe you decide to turn on some silly music to break the tension? Or maybe you ignore it, make yourself some tea, and let them figure it out? The point is, what can you do in that moment to make it better?

What if you want to binge-watch a show for 5 hours? Then, in theory, you just do it. Eventually, you'll get bored and want to do something else. And you don't know where that might lead you, but you get to feel good in the process. That might sound crazy, but I know constantly doing what you don't want to do hasn't exactly led us to any good places.

This isn't to say you should ignore your responsibilities. There are things we need to do. No one's saying get up in the middle of a work meeting and start dancing because you feel like it. But what if you could do something in that boring work meeting to make yourself feel better, even if just a little?

I've decided to make this a priority—asking myself, "What would make me feel better right now?" or "What am I most drawn to right now?" It's not a habit yet, and I do forget, but that's okay. I keep reminding myself to ask. Sometimes it looks like wanting a matcha latte or iced coffee and thinking, "Do I really need that?" But then remembering that, in the moment, that's what feels best.

We'll see where this leads me!

Update: I have been thinking a lot about manifestation. And I have come to an interesting conclusion. A lot of teachers teach that when you are manifesting, you can somehow control things outside of you, even override the freewill of others. I think this takes things a bit too far, but I am open-minded and have wanted to understand what this means for a while. I have tried to get it and ultimately, I ended up disappointed that I'm doing it "wrong." This is where my realization came in. If you do the things that make you feel good, if you put yourself in the best mood possible, what happens is you carry yourself differently and you act differently. And when you do that, new opportunities open up to you. Maybe you meet the right people or carry an energy that draws the right circumstances to you, and *that* is where the magic is. Not in controlling things outside of yourself. I may be wrong and maybe I have yet to truly understand, but what I'm realizing is the key is to be truly happy within and assume that good things are coming your way. And when disappointment hits, you are more resilient and able to bounce back. This is my current understanding, it may change in time, but for now, that feels empowering as hell and makes Bashar's principle make perfect sense. It also made me understand why so many manifestation teachers are into meditation. I never understood the connection to it and manifestation but now I got it. It makes you feel good.

Another side note because I'm an overthinker, nice to meet you. If what makes you feel better in the moment is some illegal or harmful substance, I am not saying do that. I have exactly zero expertise on the matter, so I'm certainly not implying doing something harmful, here. We're talking fun, lighthearted things, here! Walk, dance, sing, shake it off, whatever floats your boat.

Have Your Own Back

I absolutely love this simple concept! It's so straightforward, it almost hurts that it isn't common knowledge. It just means: when you make a decision, have your own damn back—and don't second-guess yourself!

For most of my life, I had a very similar hairstyle—sometimes a little longer, sometimes a little shorter, but always generally the same. I had been craving a big change for ages, and I always wanted a pixie cut. I discussed it with my coach, and I said I was afraid I'd regret it. She said something like, "Then decide you won't, and have your own back."

She went on to explain that we make decisions based on the information we have at the moment. Later, we often look back and think, "No, I shouldn't have done that!" But that's just painful.

Just like we get to decide on so many things, we also get to decide that we made the best choice in the moment—and then hold onto that decision. The flip-flopping and chastising ourselves isn't helping anyone!

I did end up getting the pixie cut, and now that my hair is growing back, I can say that I prefer it longer, at least in a short bob style. But honestly, it was a welcome change. Sometimes I had the thought that maybe it wasn't the best choice, but then I said, "NO! It was! I had so many reasons for making the decision, so good for me!"

It's really that simple, isn't it? Isn't that beautiful?

This might be the shortest chapter, but what more is there to say?

If you've ever made a decision that you later regretted, remember to have your own back, just like you would for a friend. Remind yourself why you made that decision and why it was the right one at the time—because it was. There's no other option here.

So from now on, when you make a decision, jump in with both feet! This applies to future decisions, too. If you're struggling to decide, know that whatever you decide is the right decision.

As a mom, I've had to make a lot of decisions about work—how many hours to work, whether I should work at all, whether I'm working too much or too little, etc. I need to keep reminding myself that after careful consideration, whatever I decide is correct. Period.

This doesn't mean you never reevaluate or make a new decision, but you don't look back. You know that whatever you choose is it.

If you're doubting this advice, consider the alternative: You make a decision, then go back and forth for ages. You torture yourself with "I should've, would've, could've." You lose sleep, and ask yourself why you did it the way you did. What does all that accomplish? Nothing.

The lesson here: Have your own back, no matter what you decide.

Gratitude

Gratitude. It's often mentioned and just as often forgotten. Every self-help book and guru has talked about it, but there's a reason for that. This isn't something I learned from my life coach, but it's a lesson I often forget. Manifestation coaches talk about it all the time, too.

Let's walk through two perspectives.

Perspective 1:
I wake up (in the morning feelin' like P. Diddy…what? You didn't immediately hear that song in your head like I did when you read that? Then a Millennial you are not.) and look around my room.

It's all messy. Ugh. I hear the kids screaming and feel instantly annoyed. I go downstairs to make breakfast but can't decide what to make. I'm frustrated that it's always me making breakfast. The kids are calling from the other room, needing help or arguing. More annoyance creeps in. It's the start of my day, and all I feel is frustration.

Perspective 2:

I wake up and look around my room. I see how much stuff I have and think about how lucky I am to be able to buy things for myself. I hear the kids screaming and think, "That's an opportunity to teach them about sharing." I go downstairs to make breakfast, appreciating how many choices we have. The kids call from the other room, and I either go help them or ask them to wait, seeing it as a chance for them to practice patience. I think about the fun plans we have for the day and how I can also fit in things I enjoy.

Same morning, same events, but a completely different point of view. My personal default, I hate to admit, is the first. I have to work hard to let that go. But when I do, the outcome is vastly different.

I don't think it's realistic to expect that every time your kids argue, you'll view it as an opportunity. And of course, you'll be annoyed sometimes. But the overall outlook can shift.

I often look at our house and feel frustrated by the clutter. But then I remind myself that I have the opportunity to buy so many things and decide what I want to keep—and not everyone gets that.

Even thinking about that now makes my heart feel lighter. It's so easy to focus on how tired you are and how hard motherhood can be. Sometimes, I think it's healthy to acknowledge those challenges. We should share the hard parts and not sugarcoat our lives. But at the same time, we can continue to be grateful for what we have.

You can even be grateful for the things you don't have *yet* but will in the future. This is a manifestation technique often used, and whether or not you believe in manifestation, it feels amazing! Imagining your future self and feeling gratitude for it is a fantastic experience. Gratitude is linked to all kinds of benefits, like greater life satisfaction. It's free, available at all times, and there no downsides.

Gratitude doesn't mean ignoring things that need to be changed. For example, you might be grateful for the house you live in while also looking for a new one with more of the things you desire. Maybe you have a friend who has great qualities, but they drain your energy. That's not a reason to stay in a friendship—it would be what I call toxic positivity, and that's definitely not the vibe we're going for.

You should also be aware that if you're not used to practicing gratitude and seeing the positive, there will be a learning curve. This doesn't come naturally to me, and sometimes it feels forced. Some days, it's hard to find the positive, and sometimes I feel like I'm lying to myself. But that depends on the mood I'm in at the moment.

Generally speaking, it's tough to pivot your mood on the spot. I'd suggest having something in mind that you know will make you feel better in those tough moments. Earlier in this book, I listed things that help me shift my mood once I've processed my feelings but still feel "off." But if you must force it, then force it! Finding something to be grateful for can make things feel less bleak and less overwhelming.

In our culture, gratitude is often thrown around, but I wouldn't say it gets enough attention. If you don't know where to start, you can grab a gratitude journal from pretty much anywhere. It'll help guide you and get you into the habit of regularly writing down things you're grateful for. I also recently started a list on my phone called, "Good Things Are Always Happening to Me," where I write down the good things that happened each day. This trains my mind to find the good, not the bad. That's a habit that will help anyone and everyone.

Gratitude literally changes your brain and the way you see things. How cool is that?

Stop "Shoulding" All Over the Place

This is a fun phrase, isn't it? I'm not sure if I first heard it from my coach or from *The F*ck It* Diet by Caroline Dooner (a must-read, in my opinion), but either way, I love saying it!

It's time to throw out your manual on how things "should" be.

I was talking to an acquaintance I don't speak with much, but when she called, she wanted to share how difficult things have been for her lately. She told me she was really concerned about her son, who was feeling depressed. He's a young adult, and she thought she'd be done worrying about him by now, that she could relax. She also mentioned that since it's spring, she "should" be happy, but instead, it made her feel even more miserable that she wasn't.

There's a lot to unpack here, but let's start with the "should" part of this. We all have, what my coach calls, a "manual" for life. We believe things "should" be a certain way, and when they aren't, it causes us pain. Most of us don't even realize it. It feels like a given, just how things *are*. We think that when we give a gift, our friend "should" react a certain way, or when something happens, we "should" feel a certain way. The list of "shoulds" is endless. And we don't even realize we're doing it.

The first time I discussed this with my coach, I was completely caught off guard. I didn't expect that at all because, of course, that's how things "should" be, right? I didn't even question it—there was nothing in my mind that seemed worth questioning.

It was about my mom and how I expected her to react in a specific situation. I don't remember the exact context, but it doesn't matter. I expected her to act a certain way, and I had no control over that.

What precious resources we waste thinking about how others "should" behave—holy crap! Think about how often you have expectations for almost every situation: how things "should" go, how others "should" behave, etc. It's kind of insane. Until my coach pointed it out, I never even considered or heard of this concept. To put that in context, I've been to several therapists and read plenty of self-help books. That's why I felt so compelled to write this book—this isn't common knowledge, but it *should* be.

We do this a lot with our kids as well. We expect things to be a certain way or that they should act a certain way, and then feel so ashamed when they don't. We plan an activity, thinking they will love it, or give them a gift and expect them to jump for joy. And when they don't, we feel pain. We put in all this effort, and they *need* to appreciate it, damn it!

We also place these expectations on ourselves. As my acquaintance said, she "should" feel good because it's spring and warmer outside, and everyone is supposed to be happy in spring! Let's break this down.

You're a person who feels bad about something going on in your life. But then you think, "I shouldn't be feeling this way. I *should* be happy!" In comes the guilt. In comes the shame. And there you are, feeling even worse! This is what I like to call a "shame sandwich," which is apparently my favorite snack as I've mentioned it so many times here.

I found this quote by Kimberly Borin from the Shalem Institute, which I think illustrates this perfectly:

"Every once in a while, we find ourselves making a Shame Sandwich. You know the kind. Usually, it starts out with a layer of 'bad.' Something we feel bad about, like being late, forgetting a birthday, or leaving that cup of coffee in the microwave for three days. Then, the next thing you know, we add a layer of shame, guilt, worry, and sometimes fear. Of course, we load up on the mayonnaise and maybe even add some old, familiar stale story bread. Then, we get to serve ourselves a good old Shame Sandwich. I've used this analogy with my students. It helps to see how we pile up feelings like layers of meat on an Italian hoagie. First the anger, then the shame. First the sadness, then the shame. First the fear, then the shame, and on it goes."

This quote also brings up another point: "some old, familiar stale story bread." I'll talk about that in another chapter, but for now, let's return to the sandwich.

What my acquaintance was doing here was feeling bad about feeling bad. And sometimes, we add another layer—feeling bad about feeling bad about feeling bad. Read that three times fast if you want. I'm personally very familiar with this. When I went through coaching, I felt like I *should* no longer be feeling this way, like I should already know how to handle these situations on my own.

And guess what that led to?

If you guessed an epiphany where I suddenly understood exactly how to solve my problem and felt better right away, you'd be very wrong. Turns out, you can't shame yourself into feeling better. But you can sure shame yourself into feeling worse. And that's exactly what happened. My homework after that session was to practice noticing when that layer of "shoulds" and shame crept in.

These are two different lessons from two different coaches, but they go together spectacularly well in my opinion. They're very intertwined, as we often pile on the shame based on how we think things *should* be.

There are a few concepts in that one conversation that need further discussion, so let's move on to the next chapter!

You Are Not Responsible for Others' Feelings

This one is a tough one for me and many fellow people-pleasers. I've heard this concept many times before, but most recently, I heard it on a podcast called *The Sensitive and Soulful Show with Alissa Boyer*. If you haven't listened to it, I highly recommend it. It's an excellent resource for highly sensitive people and those looking to understand their emotions better.

In the episode, Alissa talks about how highly sensitive people often take on a lot of responsibility to avoid inconveniencing others. We'd rather deal with our own discomfort than risk having someone be upset with us.

While this resonates with highly sensitive people, I'd venture to say that most women feel this way, too. We're conditioned from a young age to think about others' feelings, which is generally good. But, like many lessons we learn in childhood, we sometimes carry them into our adult lives in ways that no longer serve us.

Imagine this:

You see that the house is a mess, and you need to clean it. You ask your husband to help with a few things. He gets up, visibly annoyed because he had other things to do. He helps, but it's clear he's unhappy. You respond in an equally annoyed tone, "Fine, I'll do it myself," and he happily goes back to what he was doing.

Does this sound familiar? If not, feel free to skip this chapter. But for everyone else, I hope this is helpful.

What's happening here is that you don't want to inconvenience your partner, so you inconvenience yourself instead. Then, resentment grows. There are certainly arguments to be made about how he should know to help without being asked, or why women often carry the mental load, or how he shouldn't have been so annoyed. I agree—this isn't an ideal scenario. But the point is, we often take on responsibility for how others feel, and that's a heavy load to carry.

In a previous chapter, I mentioned my acquaintance who was concerned about her young adult son, who was feeling lost and unclear about what to do. I completely understand why she's upset; it's a tough situation. But let's break it down.

She, as his mother, feels sad about him feeling sad. She feels depressed because he's depressed. She feels she can't relax or be happy until he is. She feels like she can't enjoy her life until his problem is solved.

This is a tough spot to be in. But what has she done? She's taken on his feelings as her own. She feels that she can't be happy until he is, and she can't enjoy life until his problem is fixed. But... is that true? I say this with no judgment because I do the same thing. But as an outside observer, it's easier to see what's happening.

Let's look at the alternative: she starts following her excitement (remember the excitement formula from previous chapters?). She begins doing what feels good to her and starts enjoying life a little more each day. She goes to the gym, takes classes she enjoys, goes out to dinner with a friend, takes a walk while listening to uplifting music.

What will be the result?

She'll feel a thousand times better, and her mood will start to lift. And maybe her son's mood will lift too because right now, they're feeding off each other's energy in a toxic cycle. She'll bring fresh, positive energy into the situation. She'll allow herself to enjoy life without waiting to fix the problem first. She'll stop feeling responsible for his feelings and his life.

He may even feel better because he was subconsciously feeling bad for making his mother feel bad and put her life on hold, who knows.

I don't know exactly what the result will be, but I do know that she'll feel a lot better and he may, too. And all she had to do was realize, "I am not responsible for his feelings."

None of us are. We are responsible only for our own feelings. Isn't that liberating?

If you're crying and someone thinks you're killing the mood, sorry, but that's not your problem to fix. If you feel like your spouse or kids will be bothered because you're asking them to take on responsibilities you've been doing, that's okay too.

I'm not talking about abusive behavior or crossing boundaries, of course. If you hurt someone physically or verbally, that's on you. But I'm talking about how we go out of our way to avoid inconveniencing others or making them feel bad at the expense of our own well-being.

This lesson is difficult for me, but I have to keep practicing it. There's a saying, "What others think of you is none of your business." I know it's deeply ingrained in us to please others, and we do have to fight against our nature to practice this, but it's worth it.

Or… you can continue trying to get others to like you, be super nice and accommodating, get trampled on, be resentful, let others' thoughts control you, and generally put yourself in a position to be very unhappy. Totally up to you!

Recognize Your Old Story

We all have stories we tell ourselves. Some are positive and uplifting, but others? Not so much. Those are the ones I'm talking about.

I once worked at an online school as a speech-language pathologist, covering a maternity leave position. The schedule was already set, and when I looked at it, I saw that it was pretty light—there was a lot of downtime between seeing kids. It was amazing! I had plenty of paid time to take walks, listen to audiobooks, and relax. Meanwhile, someone was watching my kids, so I actually had time to myself. It was incredibly relaxing.

But despite enjoying it, I also felt a sense of guilt. Why? Because I was getting paid without doing any work. That same thought pops up today when I have a bunch of kids absent but still get paid.

Does that sound insane? It is. But that's my "story" about money. Something inside me believes that money has to be hard-earned, that you must work for it, and that it's wrong to receive it without working for it. And yet, I don't want to work hard for money. But that story keeps playing in my mind.

Some people charge extraordinary amounts for their time without a second thought, believing that's their worth. Meanwhile, others feel guilty about earning any money at all. That, too, is a story.

The thing about your story is that it will keep playing over and over again until you cut that sh*t loose.

Have you ever gotten into a disagreement with someone and then started doubting yourself, questioning your facts? I've done that many times—feeling like I must be the problem, even when I was sure the other person was wrong. That's a story.

What do you do? You recognize it and let it the f*ck go.

Once we become aware of something, it's no longer subconscious.

As a writer, I'm really good at creating stories. It's all fun and games until it hurts—those negative stories we all tell ourselves create serious damage.

I'm starting a new business again, and as I registered the business name and applied for an EIN, I found myself crying and doubting myself. My husband was in the room, and I told him that this was bringing up memories of the last time I opened a business and failed. Well, it wasn't exactly a failure. I realized I didn't truly want it, and I was creating more work for myself instead of freeing up my time like I intended. But even with that realization, the old story came up, and it didn't feel good.

As I reflected on it, I felt a tight knot in my stomach—fear and shame flooded me. That's my story.

I had to talk myself through it. I reminded myself that I am a new person in every moment and that one past experience does not define my future. This business model is different, it's meant to free up time. I have a clearer vision, and I have someone to ask questions because she's already doing it. But the most important thing is that I am not my past.

This ties back to the idea of making a decision. I get to decide that I'm successful and then act like it. I can either be the confident, ballsy entrepreneur who is sure of herself or the version of me who is stuck in the past, crying over a business I didn't even want. The choice is mine, and I can send that story away. Cut it loose like a bad ex. Done. Over. Let it die. And if it resurfaces, as it inevitably will, I remind myself that it's over. It's no longer true.

And then... I get to create a new story.

Quick side note: Be prepared for the story to pop up sometimes. If you're not prepared, it can catch you off guard. When you're in a situation similar to a past experience, that old story can reemerge. I wasn't prepared, and when it came up, I believed it. Rookie mistake! It can come up again, and you can recognize it and let it go, over and over, as many times as necessary. That's the antidote to being defeated by it. Anticipate it, but don't believe it.

For me, my new story is this: *I always succeed at everything I do. Things always work out for me, and it's easy. I have amazing ideas, and when I follow through, which I always do, I get the best results imaginable. And I love it!*

This ties back to the new thoughts we want to think. (See what I did there? Full circle from the first chapter—you're welcome for the satisfaction you're feeling right now.) In manifestation, this is called an affirmation—a new thought or belief you want to embrace. The simpler and shorter, the better, because it's easier to repeat.

Maybe your new affirmation could be something like, *"Everything in my life is easy and perfect"* or *"Things always go my way."* When you adopt this belief, everything will start to look different to you.

Just like with the negative story, where you keep telling yourself something, and it keeps showing up, like, *"Why do I always attract horrible men?"*—the evidence will appear. Your mind will seek out that story. If you're still holding onto the belief that all men are horrible or that you only attract the "bad ones," you may declare that you're done with that, but you'll keep attracting the same scenario. Why? Because it's your story, and you're holding onto it.

For most of us, it's hard to believe that it's that simple: change your story, and your life changes. But think about how many times those negative stories played out, and you thought, *"This again? Why?!"* So why wouldn't the same happen with a positive story?

When I first heard this idea, I didn't understand it. And I still don't completely. One explanation I like is that it's like an algorithm. The more you focus on something, the more you get related searches. It's the same in life. The classic example is when you're car shopping. Whatever car you're considering suddenly seems to appear everywhere. That's how this works.

If you think, *"Everything is always hard for me,"* you'll only notice how often things are hard for you. You may even subconsciously seek out the difficulty. You'll make things harder than they need to be, reinforcing the belief that life is always hard.

If you believe kids are always argumentative, then that's what you'll see, and you'll argue back, further creating an argumentative environment. But what if you believed kids are easy and just need to learn how to relax? You'd probably be more relaxed, and they would be too.

This cycle continues. Our beliefs and stories shape our lives. To change our lives, we have to change the thoughts we repeat. Refer to chapter one for more on that.

Let's Wrap It Up

That's it, y'all! This guide is here for when you feel lost and need a little direction. It's not meant to be comprehensive—there's always more to be said on mindset. I'm not a Buddhist monk who's spent 50 years studying this. I'm just a parent, like you, who hasn't always been taught the tools to manage my emotions and has learned that parenthood will rough you the f up.

I hope these lessons are helpful! If you need more clarification, guidance, or just some extra support, feel free to reach out to me at krengauz@gmail.com with the subject line "More Info Please."

Thank you, and MUAH! Maybe we'll meet in person someday!

About the Author

Hi! I'm Asya, an insane mother of three who is totally thriving and clearly not in survival mode, at all. I've been learning these strategies for a few years now and still can't seem to get them to seep into my brain, which is the intent of this book. I am a speech-language pathologist by day, and an author, homeschool planner, and life coordinator by every other waking and sleeping moment. I live in the Chicago suburbs and only recently started realizing what a nice area that really is. I love traveling, but have put it off with three young kids. I look forward to getting the travel of my life back, but until then, I am learning to soothe and calm my nervous system one chapter at a time. You can reach me on Facebook via my group *The Feral Mom's Society*, which, yes, is indeed a kickass name, thanks for noticing. If you need more support, you can always send me an email, *krengauz@gmail.com*, or DM me on Facebook, I like to keep things simple. Or, if you would like a free guide to find out what the F is a "Feral Mom" anyways, here's the link! https://payhip.com/b/XfcS3

Now, go change your damn thoughts to change your life.